Signatures

Grammar Practice Book

Grade 3

HARCOURT BRACE & COMPANY

ORLANDO · ATLANTA · AUSTIN · BOSTON · SAN FRANCISCO · CHICAGO · DALLAS · NEW YORK
TORONTO · LONDON

Copyright © by Harcourt Brace & Company

All rights reserved. No part of this publication may be reproduced or transmitted in
any form or by any means, electronic or mechanical, including photocopy, recording,
or any information storage and retrieval system, without permission in writing from the publisher.

Permission is hereby granted to individual teachers using the corresponding student's textbook or kit
as the major vehicle for regular classroom instruction to photocopy complete pages from this
publication in classroom quantities for instructional use and not for resale.

Duplication of this work other than by individual classroom teachers under the conditions specified
above requires a license. To order a license to duplicate this work in greater than classroom
quantities, contact Customer Service, Harcourt Brace & Company, 6277 Sea Harbor Drive, Orlando,
Florida 32887-6777. Telephone: 1-800-225-5425. Fax: 1-800-874-6418 or 407-352-3442.

HARCOURT BRACE and Quill Design is a registered trademark of Harcourt Brace & Company.

Printed in the United States of America

ISBN 0-15-306915-5

7 8 9 10   022   2000 99

To the Teacher

This *Grammar Practice* book contains practice exercises for each Grammar lesson in WINGS and DIAMOND COVE. In addition, it contains a section that focuses on improving students' proofreading skills.

PROOFREADING MAKES PERFECT consists of sequenced exercises that help students learn to proofread more effectively for errors in punctuation, capitalization, spelling, and usage.

- In the first set of exercises for each part, the errors are identified.
- In each succeeding set of exercises, students are given fewer clues to the errors.
- Finally, students proofread sentences to find errors for which no clues are given.

You may wish to have students complete **PROOFREADING MAKES PERFECT** independently, in pairs, or in cooperative groups, discussing the corrections after students finish each section. At any time during the year, students may return to **PROOFREADING MAKES PERFECT** to refresh their proofreading skills.

Contents

PROOFREADING

Capitalization and Punctuation 2
Spelling 4
Usage 6
Putting It Together 8

GRAMMAR, USAGE, AND MECHANICS

Kinds of Sentences 12
Parts of a Sentence: Subject 14
Parts of a Sentence: Predicate 16
Common Nouns 18
Proper Nouns 20
Singular and Plural Nouns 22
More Plural Nouns 24
Singular Possessive Nouns 26
Plural Possessive Nouns 28
Singular and Plural Pronouns 30
Subject Pronouns 32
Object Pronouns 34
Adjectives 36
Articles 38
Adjectives That Compare 40
Action Verbs 42
Main and Helping Verbs 44
Present-time Verbs 46
Past-time Verbs 48
Irregular Verbs 50
More Irregular Verbs 52
The Verb *be* 54
Adverbs 56
Troublesome Words 58
More Troublesome Words 60
Commas 62
Index 64

Grammar Practice

PROOFREADING MAKES PERFECT

Name _____

Proofreading your own writing can be fun.

Correcting mistakes in grammar, spelling, usage, and punctuation will make your writing easier to read. Follow the practice exercises on these pages step by step. These steps will help you remember what to look for when you proofread.

PART 1: Capitalization and Punctuation

Step 1.
The mistakes in these sentences have been pointed out for you. Rewrite the sentences correctly.

1. have you ever visited cleveland
   (capital letter, capital letter, question mark)

   _____
   _____

2. cleveland is built on the shore of lake erie.
   (capital letter, capital letter, capital letter)

   _____
   _____

3. It s on almost every map of the United States
   (apostrophe, period)

   _____
   _____

Step 2.
Now find and correct the mistakes that are listed with each sentence. Rewrite the sentences correctly.

Find three capitalization errors and two punctuation errors.

4. did you know that san diegos' zoo is famous.

   _____
   _____

Find three capitalization errors and two punctuation errors.

5. that white, Tiger is from india

   _____
   _____

Name _____

Step 3.

Can you correct the underlined mistakes? Try writing each sentence correctly.

6. how is Paper made

_____

7. it s made from wood water and dye

_____

Step 4.

Now find the number of mistakes given for each sentence. Rewrite the sentences correctly.

Find four mistakes.
8. pats team beat lee's team

_____

Find five mistakes.
9. yes i have Seen the score

_____

Find five mistakes.
10. were Stacy tom and Mario sad.

_____

Step 5.

Now try proofreading with no clues. Rewrite each sentence correctly.

11. have you ever been to mexico

_____

12. yes i have been There twice

_____

13. my mother Aunt and uncle were born in mexico city.

_____

Grammar Practice   CAPITALIZATION AND PUNCTUATION   **3**

Name _____

PART 2: Spelling

Step 1.

The spelling mistake in each sentence is underlined. Rewrite the sentence. Choose the correct spelling from the words in parentheses ( ).

(her/here)
1. Please come hear.
   _____

(flower/flouer)
2. Look at this colorful flour!
   _____

(stem/stemm)
3. It has a long stim.
   _____

(eight/eaight)
4. It has eigth small leaves.
   _____

Step 2.

Rewrite each sentence. Correct the spelling of the underlined word.

5. There is an echo in this kave.
   _____

6. Stand bye the rocky wall.
   _____

7. Can you hear are voices coming back to us?
   _____

Name _____

Step 3.

Find one spelling mistake in each sentence. Use the clues to help you. Rewrite each sentence correctly.

Find one mistake. Look for the letters or.

8. Do you like to play bord games?
   _____

Find one mistake at the beginning of a word.

9. I got a knew game for my birthday.
   _____

Find one mistake at the end of a word.

10. Dinosaurs race around a trak.
    _____

Step 4.

Now try finding the spelling mistakes with just one clue to help you. Rewrite each sentence correctly.

Find one mistake.

11. I asked Mom to by me a guitar.
    _____

Find two mistakes.

12. I already no how to play "Twinkle, Twinkle, Littel Star."
    _____
    _____

Step 5.

Now try to find spelling mistakes without any clues to help you. Rewrite each sentence correctly.

13. Nathan turned eaight years old today.
    _____
    _____

14. All his freinds were hear.
    _____

15. He got a baseball and a pare of skates.
    _____
    _____

Grammar Practice

Step 1.

Rewrite each sentence correctly. Replace each underlined word or words with one of the choices in parentheses ( ).

Step 2.

Rewrite each sentence. Replace the underlined words with words that are used correctly. Use the clues to help you.

PART 3: Usage

(went/gone)
1. I <u>goed</u> to a scout meeting last night.

(riding/rode)
2. We <u>rided</u> to the community center.

(are/is)
3. Arturo's dad <u>am</u> the troop leader.

(Rico and I/Rico and me)
4. <u>Me and Rico</u> go to meetings together.

Use another form of the verb.
5. Last year we <u>gone</u> camping together.

Use I in the subject of a sentence.
6. <u>Rico and me</u> went to Yellowstone National Park.

Use me following a word like on.
7. It rained on <u>Rico and I</u>.

Name _____

Step 3.

Now find and correct the mistake in each sentence by yourself. Use the clue to help you. Rewrite each sentence correctly.

Use another form of the verb be.

8. The Grand Canyon are in Arizona.
   _____

Use I in the subject of a sentence.

9. My family and me traveled there last month.
   _____

The verb must match the subject of the sentence.

10. Millions visits the canyon every year.
    _____

Step 4.

Rewrite the sentences correctly. Use the clue with each sentence that tells you what kind of words to replace.

Correct the main verb.

11. Have you ever saw bighorn sheep?
    _____

Correct the verb.

12. These animals lives in the tall mountains.
    _____

Replace a pronoun. Change one article.

13. In the gift shop, Alicia and me saw an picture of bighorn sheep.
    _____
    _____

Step 5.

Now find the mistakes without clues to help you. Rewrite each sentence correctly.

14. Phuong and me draw pictures of trucks.
    _____

15. Yellow lightning bolts decorates the sides of this one.
    _____

Grammar Practice   USAGE **7**

Name _____

PART 4: Putting It Together

Step 1.

These sentences have mistakes in grammar, spelling, usage, and punctuation. Each mistake is pointed out for you. Rewrite each sentence correctly.

1. Is fairbanks the largest city in alaska.
       capital letter   *capital letter*   *question mark*

   _____

2. No Anchorage are the largest City
     comma use   *singular verb*   *lowercase letter*   *period*

   _____

3. Many, ships sale north to anchorage,
     comma use   *spelling*   *capital letter*   *period*

   _____

4. Victor and me want to visit that citie.
       subject pronoun   *spelling*

   _____

5. Victor s aunt hunt for Gold in alaska years ago.
    apostrophe   *past-tense verb*   *lowercase letter*   *capital letter*

   _____

   _____

Step 2.

Now find the mistakes that are listed with each sentence. Rewrite each sentence correctly.

Find three capitalization mistakes and one punctuation mistake.

6. my dogs Name is rascal.

   _____

Find one pronoun mistake and one punctuation mistake.

7. Rascal and me have fun together

   _____

Name _____

Find two capitalization mistakes, one punctuation mistake, and one wrong verb form.

8. we playing fetch almost every Day

_____

Find two capitalization mistakes, one missing comma, and two spelling mistakes.

9. yes Rascal loves to chase Tennis bals, to.

_____

Find two capitalization mistakes, one wrong verb form, and one spelling mistake.

10. a large Dog need exercise everey day.

_____

Find two spelling mistakes and one punctuation error.

11. Maybe a goldfish wood be a better pet four you

_____

_____

Step 3.

The mistakes in these sentences are underlined. Decide why each underlined item is wrong or what is missing. Then rewrite the sentence correctly.

12. Alligators <u>likes</u> <u>Warm</u> <u>wet</u> and swampy places<u> </u>

_____

13. <u>many</u> alligators can be <u>fond</u> in <u>florida</u>?

_____

14. <u>some</u> alligators <u>lives</u> in <u>georgia</u>, <u>two</u>.

_____

15. <u>Their</u> some of the most dangerous <u>Creatures</u> on earth.

_____

_____

16. <u>yes</u> <u>i</u> have seen <u>won</u> in a zoo.

_____

Grammar Practice — PUTTING IT TOGETHER **9**

Name _____

17. It's teeth was long sharp and shiny.

_____

Step 4.

Now try finding mistakes with just one clue to help you. Rewrite each sentence correctly.

Find five mistakes.
18. can we visits aunt ann this weekend.

_____

Find five mistakes.
19. yes we'll sea Her on sunday.

_____

Find three mistakes.
20. Max an me will go their to pick blackberries.

_____

Find three mistakes.
21. What a Great Idea you have

_____

Find three mistakes.
22. Aunt Marys house is In rochester.

_____

Find five mistakes.
23. its big warm and comfortable there

_____

Name _____

Step 5.

Now try proofreading without any clues to help you find mistakes. Rewrite each sentence correctly.

24. leon angela and Eduardo are friends
_____

25. Did they right that Report?
_____

26. yes They do it together last week?
_____

27. Its about the wolves of alaska
_____

28. leons family gone their once
_____

29. They seen many wild animal.
_____

30. do wolves live in canada, two.
_____

31. yes sum do live their.
_____

KINDS OF SENTENCES

A sentence is a group of words that tells a complete thought. The words in a sentence should be in an order that makes sense.

Begin every sentence with a capital letter, and end it with an end mark.

A statement is a sentence that tells something. Use a period (.) at the end of a statement.

A question is a sentence that asks something. Use a question mark (?) at the end of a question.

An exclamation is a sentence that shows strong feeling. Use an exclamation point (!) at the end of an exclamation.

A command is a sentence that gives an order or a direction. Use a period (.) at the end of most commands.

Name _____

A. Decide whether each sentence is a statement, a question, an exclamation, or a command. Write your answer on the line. Then add the correct end mark to each sentence. The first one has been done for you.

1. The Japanese honeysuckle is an unusual plant .
   statement

2. It was brought to North America from Asia __
   _____

3. What a beautiful smell the white flowers have __
   _____

4. Have you ever seen this plant __
   _____

5. Did you know that it is a dangerous weed __
   _____

6. Don't plant the honeysuckle in your garden __
   _____

7. The sprouts can grow more than twenty-five feet in one year __
   _____

8. They could choke all your other plants __
   _____

9. Choose a different kind of plant instead __
   _____

10. What an amazing plant that honeysuckle is __
    _____

Grammar Practice

Name _____

B. Write each group of words so that it becomes a statement, a question, an exclamation, or a command. The kind of sentence is shown in parentheses ( ). The first one has been done for you.

11. our garden is a terrible mess *(exclamation)*
Our garden is a terrible mess!

12. do you think we can clean it up *(question)*
_____

13. I will remove the weeds *(statement)*
_____

14. give me that shovel *(command)*
_____

15. wow, those weeds are huge *(exclamation)*
_____

ACTIVITY CORNER

Work with a small group. Each of you should write a funny paragraph about an amazing weed. Make up a name for your fast-growing plant. Write one statement, one question, one command, and one exclamation.

Take turns reading your funny paragraph to the group. As you read each sentence, members should tell which kind of sentence is being read.

Grammar Practice — KINDS OF SENTENCES

PARTS OF A SENTENCE: SUBJECT

Every sentence has a subject.

The subject is the part of the sentence that tells the person or thing the sentence is about.

The subject is usually at the beginning of a sentence.

Name _____

A. Read each sentence. Underline the word or words that are the subject. Then put a check mark on the right to show whether the sentence tells about a person or a thing. The first one has been done for you.

		Person	Thing
1.	<u>Ancient peoples</u> grew many kinds of apples.	✓	____
2.	Scientists have found the remains of apples in Stone Age villages.	____	____
3.	Apples are still a popular fruit.	____	____
4.	English colonists brought apples to North America.	____	____
5.	John Chapman planted thousands of apple seeds.	____	____
6.	Many apples are now grown in the state of Washington.	____	____
7.	This fruit is about 85 percent water.	____	____
8.	Apple juice is made from apples.	____	____
9.	This juice is very good for you.	____	____
10.	My friends like to drink apple juice.	____	____

Name _____

the little tree
my mother
red apples
I
the grocery store

B. Choose a subject listed in the box in the side column to complete each sentence. Rewrite the sentence on the line below. Remember to include a capital letter and an end mark. The first one has been done for you.

11. _____ are my favorite snack

Red apples are my favorite snack.

12. _____ like to bring them to school for lunch

_____

13. _____ loves sour green apples

_____

14. _____ has bins filled with apples

_____

15. _____ in my yard will grow apples someday

_____

ACTIVITY CORNER

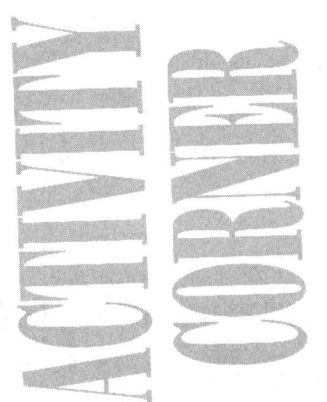

Play a game of "Subject Salad" with a partner. First, on strips of paper, each of you should write sentences that describe different fruits and vegetables. Then cut off the subject of each sentence and mix all the subjects in a bowl. Line up the other parts of the sentences on a table. Next, take turns picking a subject from the bowl. Score a point each time you can match the subject with one of the sentence parts on the table to describe correctly a fruit or vegetable.

Grammar Practice — PARTS OF A SENTENCE: SUBJECT

PARTS OF A SENTENCE: PREDICATE

Every sentence has a predicate.

The predicate is the part of the sentence that tells what the subject of the sentence is or does.

The predicate is usually the last part of the sentence.

A. Underline the subject in each sentence. Then circle the words that tell what the subject is or does. The first one has been done for you.

1. <u>New York City</u> (is the largest city in the United States.)
2. More than 7.5 million people live in New York City.
3. New Yorkers come from many different backgrounds.
4. The city has 976 public schools.
5. The subway system runs on about 230 miles of track.
6. The city is a center for trade, business, and the arts.
7. Millions visit New York City every year.
8. Theater is one of the city's most popular art forms.
9. Many visitors attend Broadway shows.
10. The city is famous for its tall buildings.
11. One of the tallest structures is the Empire State Building.
12. The Statue of Liberty stands on an island in New York Harbor.
13. This monument is a symbol of freedom.
14. Tourists take pictures of the statue.

Name _____

B. Add a predicate to complete each sentence. The first one has been done for you. If you like, you can make your sentences tell a story.

15. A duckling **waddles across the busy street.**
16. The mother duck _____
17. Cars and trucks _____
18. A police officer _____
    _____
19. The duckling _____
    _____

ACTIVITY CORNER

Write these subjects on small slips of paper.

| The elephant | An orange tiger | Two boys |
| A big tree | A mouse | A castle |

Put all the slips of paper into a hat or a box. In a group, take turns picking one slip. Read the subject out loud, and add a predicate to make a sentence. Try to build a story as you go. If you like, add other subjects and make more sentences.

Grammar Practice

COMMON NOUNS

A noun is a word that names a person, a place, or a thing.

A common noun names any person, place, or thing. It begins with a lowercase letter.

A. Circle each common noun in the paragraph. Then write the word in the chart below. The first one has been done for you. Add another paragraph and other nouns to the chart.

The (children) were getting ready for the parade. Each child stood quietly in the schoolyard. Then one boy blew a high note on his trumpet. A tall girl played her flute in the wrong key. The bandleader cried, "Get ready to march into town."

Person	Place	Thing
children		

Name _____

musician	girl
stage	tree
flute	

B. Complete each sentence with a common noun from the box at the side. Make sure your sentences make sense.

1. The sound of a _____ floated through the theater.
   (thing)

2. Another _____ began to play a horn.
   (person)

3. Then a boy appeared on the _____ .
   (place)

4. The boy hid behind a tall _____ .
   (thing)

5. A young _____ in a red dress walked onto the
   (person)
   stage.

In a small group, brainstorm common nouns that name musical instruments. Use the nouns to make a crossword puzzle. Write clues for the puzzle. Share and complete crossword puzzles with other groups.

PROPER NOUNS

A proper noun names a particular person, place, or thing.

Each important word of a proper noun begins with a capital letter.

A. Read the paragraph, and underline the proper nouns. Then write each proper noun in the web below. The first one has been done for you.

Maren wants to join the Kona Kai Swim Team, but she has a problem. She goes to Collins School on Miller Avenue. The school is three miles from the pool. That is too far for her to walk. Besides, she has to feed her dog after school. The Kona Express Bus goes only halfway to the pool. Her brother Leif has a car, but he works at the Burger Pit Restaurant until late in the evening. He can't drive her to practice.

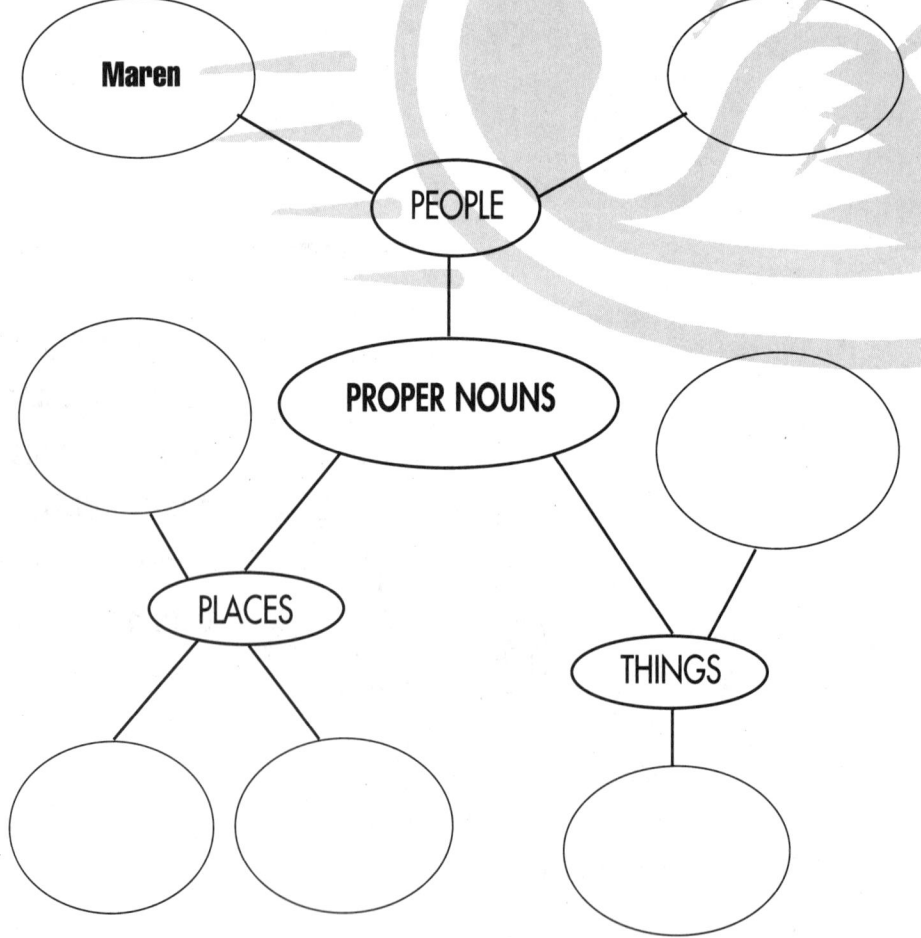

Proper Nouns — Grammar Practice

Name _____

B. Fill in the blanks with proper nouns to finish the invitation. The first one has been done for you.

Dear __**Coralia**__ ,
    (person's name)
   Hi! My name is _____ . I want to invite you to
                          (person's name)
join the _____ Club. Our next meeting is five
            (club name)
days after _____ . We usually meet every
            (particular holiday)
_____ at 3 P.M. Our clubhouse is located on
(day of the week)
_____ next to the _____
(street)   (market's name)
Market. We always have fun!

                           Your friend,

                           _____
                            (person's name)

ACTIVITY CORNER

With a partner, make or use two charts like this one to list the names of particular people, places, and things you can see or know about. Each of you should list as many proper nouns as you can in five minutes. Compare your results.

Particular Person	Particular Place	Particular Thing

Grammar Practice

SINGULAR AND PLURAL NOUNS

A singular noun names one person, one place, or one thing.

A plural noun names more than one person, place, or thing. Make most nouns plural by adding *s* or *es*.

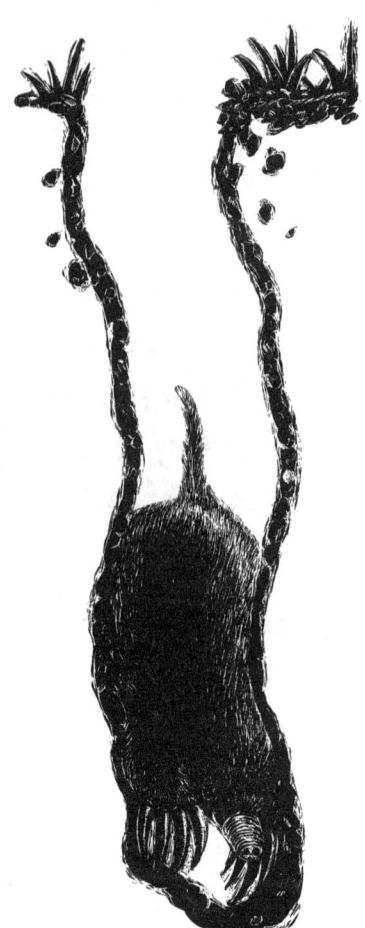

Name _____

A. Underline the nouns in these sentences. Then write the nouns in the chart where they belong. The first one has been done for you.

1. Badgers are skillful diggers.
2. A badger can dig a deep hole very quickly.
3. This mammal uses its front claws to dig.
4. A frightened animal might dig to get away from an enemy.
5. The mole also digs with powerful paws.
6. Its front legs work like shovels that scoop.
7. It digs long tunnels under bushes and trees.
8. This creature is nearly blind.
9. This furry digger does not need to see well in its dark world.

Singular Nouns	Plural Nouns
	Badgers
	diggers

Grammar Practice

Name _____

beaver	inch
stick	bush
branch	room

B. Choose a noun from the box to complete each sentence. Add *s* or *es* to each noun to make it plural.

10. Look over there in those thick green _____.

11. I see two baby _____.

12. They are gnawing on some long tree _____.

13. A beaver's teeth are about two _____ long.

14. The beavers will carry the cut _____ into the water.

15. A beaver's underwater house has many _____.

ACTIVITY CORNER

Find a book that has many pictures of a natural setting such as mountains or a swamp. Work with a partner to list in a chart the things you see. List all the singular nouns in one column of the chart. List all the plural nouns in the other. Use the nouns in your finished chart to write and illustrate a poem about your chosen place in nature.

Grammar Practice — SINGULAR AND PLURAL NOUNS

MORE PLURAL NOUNS

If a noun ends with a consonant and *y*, change the *y* to *i* and add *es* to form the plural.

Some nouns change spelling in the plural form.

Name _____

A. Complete each sentence with a word from the box. Use the clues to help you. The first one has been done for you.

goose	man	foot
geese	men	feet
mouse	child	person
mice	children	people

1. An old ___**goose**___ stopped by the side of the road.
   (bird)

2. "My _____ hurts!" she complained.
   (part of the body)

3. Two _____ passed by.
   (young people)

4. "What's the matter, Goose?" one _____ asked.
   (young person)

5. "Please rub my two tired _____," the goose
   (parts of the body)
   begged.

6. A kind _____ stopped to help.
   (grown-up boy)

7. "I will give you _____ a golden egg!" the goose
   (more than one person)
   promised.

8. "A _____ will deliver it to you tomorrow."
   (small animal)

Name _____

B. Rewrite each underlined noun. If the noun is singular, make it plural. If the noun is plural, make it singular. The first one has been done for you.

9. I like to read good <u>stories</u>. **story**
10. I keep <u>copies</u> of my favorite ones in my room. _____
11. "The Boy Who Cried Wolf" is a famous <u>story</u>. _____
12. A shepherd boy was lonely for his <u>buddies</u>. _____
13. One day he let out a <u>cry</u> of "Wolf! Wolf!" _____
14. <u>Families</u> ran to help. _____
15. The <u>child</u> had played a joke on them. _____
16. All the men and <u>women</u> were angry. _____
17. Even the other <u>children</u> did not believe him after that. _____

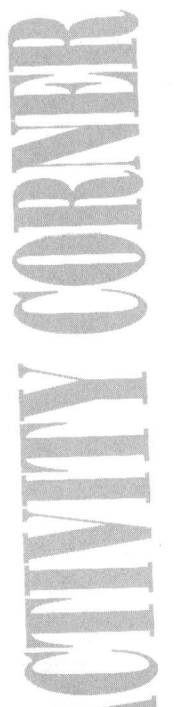

ACTIVITY CORNER

Play "Noun Hunt" with a partner.

Share your favorite book. Work together to find plural nouns in the book.

Make a list of as many plural nouns as you can. Keep score this way:

noun that adds s or es to become plural = 1 point

noun that changes y to i and adds es = 2 points

noun that changes spelling = 3 points

Grammar Practice   MORE PLURAL NOUNS **25**

SINGULAR POSSESSIVE NOUNS

A singular possessive noun shows ownership by one person or thing.

Add an apostrophe (') and *s* to a singular noun to show ownership.

A. Circle the possessive noun in each sentence. Draw an arrow from the possessive noun to the thing that belongs to it. The first one has been done for you.

1. A kayak is like a canoe, except that a (kayak's) top is covered.
2. Alaska's Inuits created kayaks thousands of years ago.
3. The kayak's frame was often made of wood.
4. The boat's covering kept water out.
5. Mari's kayak holds two people.
6. This girl's paddle is long and thin.
7. Mari likes to race through the river's rapids.
8. It takes skill to paddle through the ocean's waters.
9. Mari saw a shark's fin from far away.
10. The whale's song is musical.

26 SINGULAR POSSESSIVE NOUNS — Grammar Practice

Name _____

B. Find the possessive noun in each sentence. Decide what belongs to that person or thing. Write your answers in the chart. The first row has been done for you.

11. The man's sled traveled over ice and snow.
12. The dog's breath was a cloud of white.
13. The animal's fur kept it warm and cozy.
14. The trader's jacket was decorated with beads.
15. The sky's clouds became heavy and dark.
16. The sled raced toward the town's lights.

Possessive Noun	What Belongs
man's	sled

ACTIVITY CORNER

Imagine that you are visiting a place in the far north. Make a postcard to send to a classmate. Write about what you see and hear. Use at least two possessive nouns.

Grammar Practice — SINGULAR POSSESSIVE NOUNS **27**

PLURAL POSSESSIVE NOUNS

A plural possessive noun shows ownership by more than one person or thing.

To form the possessive of a plural noun that ends in *s*, add an apostrophe (').

Name _____

A. Rewrite each sentence. Change each singular possessive noun to a plural possessive noun. The first one has been done for you.

1. The girl's kite was made of colorful paper.
   The girls' kite was made of colorful paper.

2. Tony could hear his friend's cheers as his kite rose higher.
   _____
   _____

3. The kites danced along the cloud's fluffy edges.
   _____

4. Many birds were perched in the tree's branches.
   _____
   _____

5. The blue jay's cries could be heard all over the park.
   _____
   _____

6. The boy's dogs barked loudly at the noisy birds.
   _____

7. The twin's Frisbee sailed all the way to the baseball field.
   _____
   _____

8. The wind did not spoil the family's day at the park.
   _____
   _____

Name _____

B. Underline the possessive noun in each sentence. On the line, write whether it is *singular* or *plural*. The first one has been done for you.

9. The <u>table's</u> leg was loose. — **singular**

10. The dog's wagging tail thumped against the table. _____

11. The families' homemade cookies fell to the ground. _____

12. The picnickers' dessert was ruined! _____

13. The ripe blackberries' smell was sweet. _____

14. Danny borrowed Adam's bowl. _____

15. The children filled their grandparents' buckets with berries. _____

ACTIVITY CORNER

Work in a group to write a short news story for television. Describe an outdoor activity or sports event you know about. Use at least two plural possessive nouns. Then prepare to present your news story to your classmates.

Grammar Practice — PLURAL POSSESSIVE NOUNS

SINGULAR AND PLURAL PRONOUNS

A singular pronoun replaces a singular noun.

The words *I, me, you, he, she, him, her*, and *it* are singular pronouns.

Always capitalize the pronoun *I*.

A plural pronoun replaces a plural noun.

The words *we, you, they, us*, and *them* are plural pronouns.

A. Read each pair of sentences. Write the pronoun that fits best in the second sentence of each pair. Use the clue in parentheses ( ) to help you. The first one has been done for you.

1. Piñatas are popular in Mexico.
   __**They**__ are hollow toys made from paper.
   (plural)

2. Piñatas come in many shapes.
   Often _____ are shaped like animals.
   (plural)

3. The piñata hangs from the ceiling.
   _____ contains gifts and treats.
   (singular)

4. Anita tries to hit the piñata with a stick.
   _____ has been blindfolded.
   (singular)

5. The children cheer when the piñata breaks.
   _____ rush to collect the prizes.
   (plural)

6. Our teacher, Mr. Pettway, handed out balloons.
   _____ explained how to make piñatas.
   (singular)

7. All of us covered a balloon with strips of wet newspaper.
   _____ left a hole at the end of the balloon.
   (plural)

8. Ben decorated the piñata.
   "Please hand _____ the red paint," Kevin said.
   (singular)

9. The boys popped the balloon.
   _____ poured treats into the hole and closed the opening.
   (plural)

Name _____

I	me	you
he	she	him
her	it	we
us	they	them

B. Rewrite each sentence. Choose a pronoun from the box to replace the underlined word or words. The first sentence has been rewritten for you.

10. After school, <u>Jasmine</u> went to the playground.
    After school, she went to the playground.

11. <u>Some children</u> were sledding down the hill.
    _____

12. Jasmine ran home to get <u>a sled</u>.
    _____

13. <u>Mrs. Joseph</u> told her daughter to stay warm.
    _____

14. Jasmine's sister Thea asked to go with <u>Jasmine</u>.
    _____

ACTIVITY CORNER

Make a snow mobile, or hanging sculpture, that uses pronouns. Make three paper snowflakes. Write one sentence on each snowflake about a favorite winter activity. On the opposite side of each snowflake, write another sentence about the same topic using a singular or plural pronoun. Use string to hang your snowflakes from a coat hanger.

SUBJECT PRONOUNS

A subject pronoun takes the place of one or more nouns in the subject of a sentence.

The words *I*, *you*, *he*, *she*, *it*, *we*, and *they* are subject pronouns.

Name _____

A. Replace the word or words in parentheses ( ) with a subject pronoun. Remember to begin each sentence with a capital letter. The first one has been done for you.

1. (Gloria and Steven) __**They**__ went to the beach.
2. (The shore) _____ was lined with shells.
3. (Gloria) _____ found a starfish.
4. (Steven) _____ picked up a long strand of seaweed.
5. "Will (Gloria) _____ carry my bucket of shells?" Steven asked Gloria.
6. "(Steven) _____ want to jump in the waves," Steven explained.
7. "(Steven and Gloria) _____ should return these shells to the beach," Gloria said.
8. "(The shells) _____ belong here," she continued.
9. (Steven) _____ agreed.
10. (The starfish) _____ was Gloria's favorite beach discovery.

32 SUBJECT PRONOUNS — Grammar Practice

Name _____

B. Read each pair of sentences. Circle the subject pronoun in the second sentence. Tell what word or words the subject pronoun replaces. The first one has been done for you.

11. The Petersens went camping. (They) took sleeping bags and tents.
    The Petersens _____

12. Gloria wanted to set up the tent alone. She didn't hammer the stakes in well.
    _____

13. The tent fell down. It looked funny lying in the dirt.
    _____

14. "Mary, please help your sister," Mom said. "You know how to set up the tent."
    _____

15. Mary and Gloria tried again. They put the tent up right.
    _____

ACTIVITY CORNER

With a partner, write these subject pronouns on slips of paper. Turn the slips over. Take turns choosing a pronoun to begin a sentence. Make up a story as you go!

| I | you | he | she |

| it | we | they |

Grammar Practice — SUBJECT PRONOUNS

OBJECT PRONOUNS

An object pronoun follows an action verb, such as *see* or *tell*, or a word such as *about, at, for, from, near, of, to,* or *with.*

The words *me, you, him, her, it, us,* and *them* are object pronouns.

Name _____

A. Rewrite the sentences. Replace the underlined word or words with an object pronoun. The first one has been done for you.

1. Emily and Raoul took the ferry north.
   Emily and Raoul took it north.

2. The ferry carried Emily and Raoul to Alaska.
   _____

3. Emily pointed her camera at Raoul.
   _____

4. "Look at Emily," Emily said.
   _____

5. The coastline was not far from Raoul and Emily.
   _____

6. Raoul saved a deck chair for Emily.
   _____

7. Raoul and Emily looked over the railing at the dolphins.
   _____

8. "Do you think the dolphins notice Emily and Raoul?" Raoul asked Emily.
   _____

Name _____

B. Underline the object pronoun in the second sentence in each pair. Write the object pronoun on the line. Also, write the word or words the pronoun replaces. The first one has been done for you.

	Object Pronoun	What It Replaces
9. The children saw a bald eagle. The children watched <u>it</u> fly.	it	a bald eagle
10. The ranger spoke to the children. The ranger told them that the eagle is endangered.	_____	_____
11. Too much hunting and pollution hurt the eagles. Now the government protects them with stronger laws.	_____	_____
12. The children drew pictures. "The eagle is a symbol of freedom to us," Emily said.	_____	_____

ACTIVITY CORNER

Make a poster about a wild animal you would like to help in nature. Write a sentence or two under your picture. Use an object pronoun.

Grammar Practice — Object Pronouns

ADJECTIVES

An adjective is a word that describes a noun.

Some adjectives tell *how many*.

Some adjectives tell *what kind*.

Name _____

A. Write each adjective. Write whether it tells *how many* or *what kind*. (Do not write the words *a*, *an*, and *the*.) The first one has been done for you.

1. A big tree grows in the yard.
   big—what kind

2. I often gaze up into the huge branches.
   _____

3. One bird has built a little nest there.
   _____

4. The nest has three speckled eggs in it.
   _____

5. Many animals visit the tree.
   _____

6. A small squirrel collects fat acorns.
   _____

7. Two black crows land on a branch.
   _____

8. Some creatures depend on the old tree.
   _____

Name _____

beautiful	heavy
tiny	small
many	hungry
white	frightened
big	bare
rough	warm

B. Complete the sentences with one or more adjectives from the box. Remember to begin each sentence with a capital letter. The first sentence has been done for you.

9. ___Beautiful___ flowers bloom beneath the ___big___ tree.

10. When _____ rain falls, _____ animals hide in the tree.

11. _____ insects crawl on the _____ bark.

12. _____ birds eat them.

13. In winter, _____ snow falls on the tree's _____ branches.

14. _____ creatures sleep during winter.

15. A _____ squirrel makes a _____ home in the tree.

ACTIVITY CORNER

Cut out some pictures of animals from old magazines. Paste the pictures on a sheet of paper to make a collage.

Underneath each picture, write an adjective and a noun that tell about the picture.

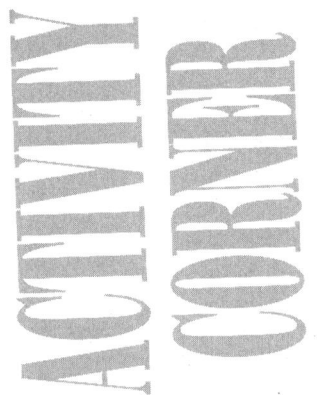

Grammar Practice

ARTICLES

The adjectives *a*, *an*, and *the* are called articles.

Use *a* before a word that begins with a consonant sound.

Use *an* before a word that begins with a vowel sound.

Use *the* before a word that begins with a consonant or a vowel.

A. Complete each sentence by writing *a*, *an*, or *the*. The first one has been done for you.

1. I have ____**a**____ comic book collection.
2. I keep my comics in _____ special place.
3. They are stored in _____ attic of our house.
4. Each comic book tells _____ story.
5. My favorite comic is about _____ emperor.
6. He lives in _____ castle made of ice.
7. _____ ice never melts.
8. His castle is on _____ island.
9. _____ emperor solves mysteries from his castle.
10. The emperor has _____ enemy named Grog.
11. Grog is _____ foolish character.
12. I could read comics for _____ hour at a time!

Name _____

a	adventure
an	air
the	superhero
	island
	tiger

B. Complete each sentence with an article and a noun from the box. The first one has been done for you.

13. Iron Lady always loves ____an____ ____adventure____.
14. She can fly through _____ _____ very fast.
15. She is _____ _____.
16. She lives on _____ _____ in the sea.
17. She keeps _____ _____ as a pet.

ACTIVITY CORNER

Invent a superhero of your own.

Draw a picture of your hero.

Write some sentences telling about your hero's special powers. Circle the articles you use.

Share your drawing and sentences with classmates.

Grammar Practice ARTICLES **39**

ADJECTIVES THAT COMPARE

Name _____

Adjectives can describe by comparing people, animals, places, or things.

Add **-er** to most adjectives to compare two things.

Add **-est** to most adjectives to compare more than two things.

Some adjectives need the word *more* or *most* for comparing.

Use *more* with an adjective to compare two things.

Use *most* with an adjective to compare more than two things.

A. Fill in each blank with an adjective from the box. The first one has been done for you.

sweeter	heavier	juicier
sweetest	heaviest	juiciest
bigger	redder	riper
biggest	reddest	ripest

1. Oranges are sweet, but cherries are **sweeter**.
2. I think watermelons are the _____ fruit of all.
3. This pink grapefruit is heavy, but that yellow one is even _____.
4. This strawberry is the _____ one I have ever seen!
5. Cherry pits are _____ than apple seeds.
6. I will choose the _____ peach in the basket for my lunch.
7. This orange is even _____ than the one I ate yesterday.
8. Let's find the _____ watermelon in the garden.
9. Is this one _____ than that one?
10. The ripest melon will be the _____ melon.

Name _____

B. Write *more* or *most* in each blank. The first one has been done for you.

11. Warm apple pie has the ___**most**___ wonderful smell in the world!

12. Uncle Jasper's apple pie is even _____ delicious than Dad's.

13. Uncle Jasper is the _____ talented baker of all in our family.

14. His peach pie is _____ flavorful than mine.

15. He uses the _____ unusual recipes of anyone I know.

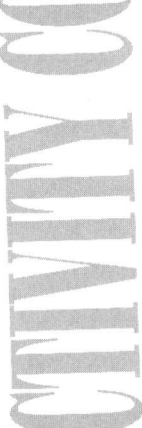

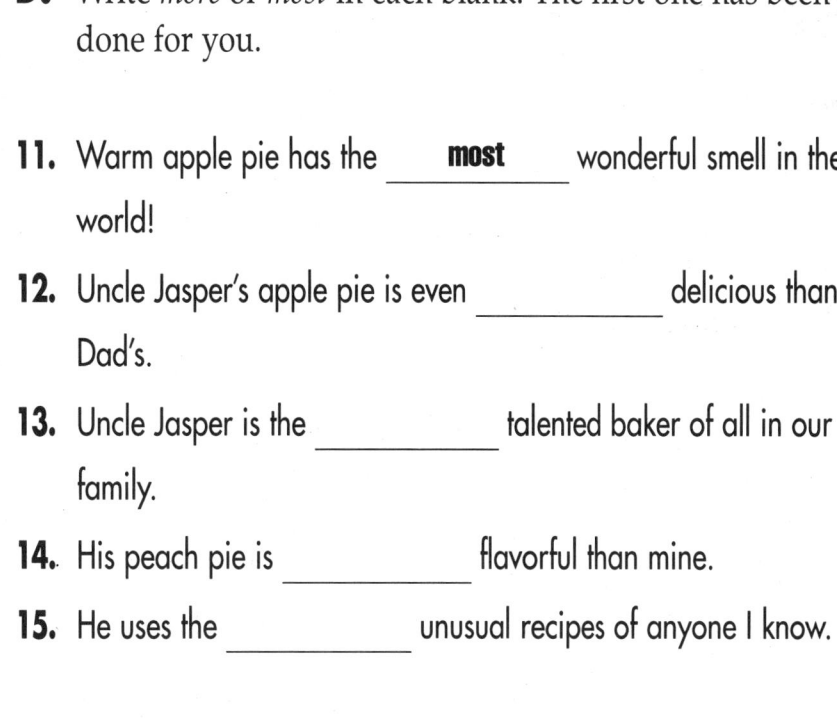

Work in a group to draw three pies. Then imagine that you are judging the three pies. Use the words *juicy, delicious, flaky, spicy,* and *beautiful* to compare the pies. Take turns writing a sentence that compares the pies. Pick the winning pie, and draw a picture of a blue ribbon on it.

ACTION VERBS

An action verb is a word that shows action.

An action verb is the main word in the predicate of a sentence.

An action verb is a word that tells what the subject of a sentence does.

A. Read each sentence. Write the action verb. The first one has been done for you.

1. I peek through the curtains at the yard. _____peek_____
2. The snow covers the ground with a thick white blanket. _____
3. Eagerly I go outside. _____
4. I close the door quickly behind me. _____
5. I walk in the freezing air. _____
6. My feet crunch in the new snow. _____
7. The cold wind nips my nose. _____
8. I build a huge snowman. _____
9. Then I return to my warm house. _____
10. I remove my coat and mittens. _____
11. I make a cup of hot chocolate. _____
12. I drink it by the fire. _____

Name _____

eat	dive
read	throw
talk	draw
run	swim
splash	catch
slide	play
paint	

B. Write a sentence telling what you do at each place listed below. Use an action verb from the box. The first one has been done for you.

13. a restaurant
   I eat at a restaurant.

14. the beach
   _____

15. a friend's house
   _____

16. the art room
   _____

17. the playground
   _____

18. a baseball field
   _____

1. Work in a group to make a guessing game. Each of you should find in a magazine a picture that shows people doing something.

2. Cut out the picture and paste it on a piece of cardboard.

3. On each of three index cards, write an action verb that tells what the people in your picture are doing. Mix your verb cards in with everyone else's.

4. Take turns choosing a verb card, reading the action verb out loud, and trying to guess which picture the action verb goes with.

Grammar Practice

MAIN AND HELPING VERBS

The main verb is the most important verb in a sentence.

A helping verb can work with the main verb to tell about an action. The helping verb always comes before the main verb.

The words *have, has,* and *had* are often used as helping verbs.

A. Complete each sentence. Write a helping verb and a main verb from the box. Then circle the main verb. You can use words more than once. The first one has been done for you.

Helping Verbs

have   has   had

Main Verbs

| delivered | ordered | baked | brought |
| invited | waited | decorated | covered |

1. My dad ___has___ ___(baked)___ my birthday cake.
2. He _____ _____ the cake with little candles.
3. By last week I _____ _____ all my friends to my party.
4. They _____ _____ presents for me.
5. I _____ _____ for my birthday all year.
6. My mother _____ _____ the house with balloons.
7. We _____ _____ two large pizzas.
8. The mail carrier _____ _____ a big birthday package from my grandma in Detroit.

44   MAIN AND HELPING VERBS   *Grammar Practice*

Name _____

B. Underline each verb. Then write each verb on the line. Label it *helping* or *main*.

9. My father had wrapped my present the night before.

   _____

10. He had built a wooden box for my rock collection.

    _____

11. My grandfather has mailed me some new and unusual rocks.

    _____

12. I have liked rocks for a long time.

    _____

ACTIVITY CORNER

Work in a group. Imagine that you have planned a surprise party for a friend. Say three sentences, telling about the preparations you have made. Use a helping verb and a main verb in each sentence. Here is an example:

"I have made an apple cake."

The other group members can stop you if you forget to use both a helping verb and a main verb. Then the next player takes a turn.

Grammar Practice — MAIN AND HELPING VERBS

PRESENT-TIME VERBS

A present-time verb tells about action that happens now.

The form of the verb depends on the subject of the sentence. Add *s* or *es* to most present-time verbs when the subject of the sentence is *he*, *she*, *it*, or a singular noun.

Do not add *s* or *es* to a present-time verb when the subject is *I*, *you*, *we*, *they*, or a plural noun.

A. Complete each sentence with a present-time verb from the box. The first one has been done for you.

drive	take	play
drives	takes	plays
drink	chase	watch
drinks	chases	watches

1. My grandparents __drive__ to our vacation cabin in the north.
2. My aunt _____ her car there, too.
3. I _____ icy lemonade.
4. Mom _____ iced tea.
5. Eddie and I _____ catch.
6. Then we _____ each other around the yard.
7. Our dog Mondo _____ us silently.
8. He _____ the ball from us.
9. Alicia _____ a game of checkers with Mom.
10. Mondo _____ after a ball I have thrown.
11. We _____ the sun go down.
12. Later, it _____ us one hour to drive home.

46 PRESENT-TIME VERBS   *Grammar Practice*

Name _____

B. Choose the correct present-time verb in each sentence. The first one has been done for you.

13. In the summer I (travel/travels) to my cousins' house. **travel**
14. My cousins (live/lives) on a farm. _____
15. Uncle Abe (grow/grows) corn there. _____
16. We (ride/rides) Clancy, the old farm horse. _____
17. We (swim/swims) in an icy creek. _____
18. Sometimes at night we (build/builds) a campfire. _____
19. Uncle Abe (tell/tells) stories. _____
20. In the winter my cousins (visit/visits) me. _____

ACTIVITY CORNER

Picture in your mind the perfect Saturday. Draw pictures of five things you could do on this day. Then exchange papers with a partner. Write a sentence telling what happens in each picture. Use present-time verbs.

Grammar Practice — PRESENT-TIME VERBS

PAST-TIME VERBS

A past-time verb shows action that happened in the past.

Add *ed* or *d* to most present-time verbs to make them show past time.

A. Write the past-time verb from each sentence on the line. Circle the ending that makes the verb show past time. The first one has been done for you.

1. It rained last night.   rain(ed)
2. We closed all the windows quickly. _____
3. Thunder crashed outside. _____
4. The dog barked at the loud noise. _____
5. I watched the lightning. _____
6. Rain poured from the roof. _____
7. The roof leaked in two places. _____
8. We placed buckets under the leaks. _____
9. My mother started a fire in the fireplace. _____
10. We heated some apple cider. _____
11. We shared a bowl of popcorn. _____
12. We listened to the storm. _____

48 PAST-TIME VERBS   Grammar Practice

Name _____

melt	play
skate	snow
	cover

B. Complete each sentence with the past-time form of a verb from the box. First, think of the ending that makes each verb show past time. Then write the past-time verb on the line.

13. Last winter it _____ heavily.
14. The snow _____ the ground.
15. We _____ in the snow.
16. I _____ on the frozen pond.
17. My snowman _____ in the sun.

ACTIVITY CORNER

Draw a scene that shows you and a friend working in a garden. Your scene can show sun, wind, rain, snow, or any other kind of weather. Then write sentences under the picture. Tell what happened. Your sentences should use past-time verbs to show that the action happened in the past.

Grammar Practice

IRREGULAR VERBS

An irregular verb is a verb that does not end with *ed* to show past time.

A. Choose the correct past-time verb in parentheses ( ) to complete each sentence. Write the verb on the line. The first one has been done for you.

1. Yesterday Brian (drives/drove) the tractor past his vegetable garden. _____**drove**_____

2. He (have/had) no more vegetables. _____

3. He (gone/went) past a small hole in the ground. _____

4. A friendly rabbit (gave/gives) him a wink. _____

5. The rabbit said, "You (comed/came) on a lovely sunny day!" _____

6. "You (ate/eaten) almost all of my food!" Brian exclaimed. _____

7. Brian (give/gave) the rabbit new seeds to plant. _____

8. The rabbit (done/did) a lot of hard work. _____

came	gone	ate
come	went	eaten
did	done	gave

B. Complete each sentence with a past-time verb from the box. The first sentence has been done for you.

Dear Brian,

Last week I ____**went**____ to a Rabbit Reunion. Some of the rabbits _____ from very far away. We _____ carrots and cucumbers. I _____ a speech. I said that since we have _____ to the farm and eaten food, we must help the farmers plant some more. Some of the rabbits did not agree. I _____ my best to convince them, though.

Love,
Rabbit

ACTIVITY CORNER

Draw a comic strip about Brian and Rabbit. Try to use the past-time forms of these verbs:

come   go   do   give   eat

Grammar Practice — IRREGULAR VERBS

MORE IRREGULAR VERBS

An irregular verb is a verb that does not end with *ed* to show past time.

Name _____

A. Write the correct past-time form of the verb in parentheses ( ). The first one has been done for you.

1. At the fair last summer we (ride) __**rode**__ on the giant Ferris wheel.
2. I (see) _____ our house a mile away!
3. Later my brother (take) _____ my Red Sox cap from me.
4. I (run) _____ after him and got the cap back!
5. My brother (think) _____ he was funny.
6. I have always (have) _____ a great sense of humor.
7. I (say) _____ to him, "Someday I will be a circus clown."
8. I have (take) _____ tumbling classes.
9. My coach has (say) _____ many times that I have talent.
10. My parents have (see) _____ me in action, and they agree.

Name _____

B. Rewrite the sentences. Choose a word in parentheses ( ) to make each sentence tell about the past.

11. The circus performers (ridden/rode) the train into town.
    _____

12. Setting up the circus tent has (take/taken) a lot of work.
    _____
    _____

13. Everyone has (had/have) to do several chores.
    _____

14. The monkeys (ran/runs) around until the trainer called them.
    _____
    _____

ACTIVITY CORNER

1. In a group, brainstorm a list of irregular verbs. Write the present-time form of each irregular verb on a separate index card.

2. Trade cards with another group.

3. Take turns drawing a card and spelling the past-time form of the verb. Use each verb form in a sentence. Score a point for each correctly used verb form.

Grammar Practice   MORE IRREGULAR VERBS

THE VERB BE

Forms of the verb *be* link the subject of the sentence to one or more words in the predicate. They tell what or where someone or something is or was.

The subject and the form of the verb *be* should agree.

Am, is, and *was* are used with singular subjects.

Are and *were* are used with plural subjects and with the subject *you.*

A. Complete each sentence. Write a form of the verb *be* from the box in each blank. The first one has been done for you.

am	was
are	were
is	

1. The clouds ___were___ thick last night.
2. The stars _____ hidden.
3. I _____ not able to see them.
4. Tonight the stars _____ bright.
5. I _____ happy to see them.
6. One star _____ blue in color.
7. Its name _____ Sirius.
8. Sirius _____ the brightest star in the sky.

Name _____

B. Rewrite each sentence. Choose the correct form of the verb *be* from the words in parentheses ( ).

9. Yesterday I (were/was) at Morgan's house.
   _____

10. A show about the night sky (was/were) on TV.
    _____

11. Planets and stars (is/are) different.
    _____

12. Mars (were/is) reddish in color.
    _____

13. Compared to the planets, I (are/am) very small!
    _____

ACTIVITY CORNER

Make a drawing of the solar system. Draw the nine planets that move around the sun. Write a sentence below each planet. You might answer these questions:

Which planet is closest to the sun?

Which planets are farthest from the sun?

Which is the largest planet?

Use forms of the verb *be* in your sentences.

Grammar Practice

ADVERBS

An adverb is a word that describes a verb.

An adverb may tell *where*, *when*, or *how* an action happens.

A. In the space after each sentence, write the adverb. Then write whether each adverb tells *when*, *where*, or *how* the action happened. The first one has been done for you.

	Adverb	When, Where, or How?
1. Yesterday my family went on a hike.	Yesterday	when
2. We ate our picnic lunch hungrily.		
3. Later we played hide-and-seek.		
4. My brother hid nearby in a cave.		
5. He screamed loudly.		
6. Quickly we ran to the cave.		
7. We saw some bats there.		
8. They slept peacefully.		
9. We left the cave quietly.		
10. My brother looked nervously over his shoulder.		

Name _____

swiftly	always
carefully	there
silently	sometimes

B. Write an adverb from the box in each blank below. Use the clues for help. The first one has been done for you.

11. __Sometimes__ we go mountain climbing.
    (when—not all the time)

12. We check our equipment _____ before we begin.
    (how—taking no chances)

13. We climb _____ to the peak.
    (how—fast)

14. We eat our lunch _____ .
    (where—in that place)

15. We _____ clean up our trash.
    (when—every time)

16. We watch a hawk gliding _____ in the air.
    (how—without noise)

ACTIVITY CORNER

Work with a partner. Imagine that you are travel agents. Plan and make a travel brochure that uses adverbs to advertise a mountain-climbing trip.

TROUBLESOME WORDS

Use *to* when you mean "in the direction of."

Use *too* when you mean "also."

Use *two* when you mean the number.

Use *your* when you mean "belonging to you."

Use *you're* when you mean "you are."

Name _____

A. Complete each sentence. Write the word in parentheses ( ) that belongs in the sentence. The first one has been done for you.

1. I went (to/too/two) the beach with my family. __**to**__
2. I found (to/too/two) shells. _____
3. Ramón found some shells, (to/too/two). _____
4. Did you bring (your/you're) flippers? _____
5. (Your/You're) going to need them. _____
6. Yes, I brought (to/too/two) pairs. _____
7. Some divers are swimming over (to/too/two) the rocks. _____
8. Is (you're/your) brother with them? _____
9. Carlo is diving, (to/too/two). _____
10. Look! They caught (to/too/two) fish! _____

Name _____

B. Rewrite each sentence. Correct the underlined word so that it is spelled correctly. Use the words in the box to help you.

two	to	too
your	you're	

11. I see <u>too</u> crabs in the water.

    _____

12. I see a sea snail, <u>to</u>.

    _____

13. Did you bring <u>you're</u> net?

    _____

14. Let's take it <u>two</u> the tide pool.

    _____

15. <u>Your</u> being very careful.

    _____

16. Return each creature <u>too</u> its home.

    _____

ACTIVITY CORNER

With a partner, write a story about two divers at a beach. Take turns using words from the box in Part B to write sentences for your story. Share your story with classmates.

MORE TROUBLESOME WORDS

Use *its* when you mean "belonging to it."

Use *it's* when you mean "it is."

Use *there* when you mean "in that place."

Use *their* when you mean "belonging to them."

Use *they're* when you mean "they are."

Name _____

A. Complete each sentence. Write the word in parentheses ( ) that belongs in the sentence. The first one has been done for you.

1. (There/Their/They're) pointing to a star. __They're__
2. What is (its/it's) name? _____
3. (Its/It's) called the North Star. _____
4. (Its/It's) easy to find. _____
5. Look up (there/their/they're)! _____
6. For travelers, (its/it's) the most important star in the sky. _____
7. (Its/It's) the star that shows where North is. _____
8. It can help people find (there/their/they're) way home. _____
9. What are those stars over (there/their/they're) called? _____
10. (There/Their/They're) called the Big Dipper. _____

Name _____

its	there
it's	their
	they're

B. Read each riddle. Write the correct word from the box in each blank. Remember to capitalize the first word in a sentence. Then write the answer. The first one has been done for you.

11. __**They're**__ crafts that astronauts ride in. __**Their**__ engines are very powerful. Millions watch __**their**__ takeoffs. Look __**there**__ to your left to see one. What are they?

    They're spaceships.

12. _____ something that keeps us warm. _____ rays shine down and give us light. _____ very hot. What is it?

    _____

13. _____ are many of these in the night sky. _____ small and bright. _____ hard to count them all. What are they?

    _____

14. Twice a month _____ a big, bright circle. Then _____ shape changes to a slim curve. Finally, it disappears. Astronauts have landed _____. What is it?

    _____

ACTIVITY CORNER

Think of another riddle. Write three clues. Use some of the words from the box in Part B in your clues. Give your riddle to a friend to solve.

Grammar Practice — MORE TROUBLESOME WORDS

COMMAS

Use a comma (,) to set off the words *yes, no,* and *well* at the beginning of a sentence.

Use a comma after each item except the last one in a series of three or more items.

A. Rewrite each sentence. Add commas where they belong. The first one has been done for you.

1. An octopus has eight legs large eyes and strong jaws.
   An octopus has eight legs, large eyes, and strong jaws.

2. No this octopus is not large.

3. Well most octopuses are only as big as a fist.

4. Yes an octopus can change color.

5. It can become blue purple red or white.

6. An octopus eats clams crabs and lobsters.

7. Octopuses live along the coasts of Hawaii Australia and China.

8. Yes they live in warm waters.

Name _____

B. Read the paragraph. Add the thirteen missing commas where they belong.

Lisa Jay and Jeanelle went to the aquarium. The aquarium was cool dark and quiet. They saw a seahorse an octopus and a shark. Yes they were glad that the creatures were in a tank! The octopus held onto the glass the wall and a rock. No the three friends did not see any whales. They bought a book a poster and a hat in the gift shop. Yes it was a good day.

ACTIVITY CORNER

1. **Imagine that you are a famous scientist. You will be interviewed on television about sea animals. The reporter has given you these questions ahead of time.**

   What are your favorite sea animals? Name three animals.
   Have you ever seen them in the wild?
   How can you learn about sea animals? Name three ways.
   Would you want a sea creature as a pet? Why or why not?

2. **Write a complete sentence that answers each question. Each sentence should use a series comma or an introductory comma.**

3. **Have a classmate ask you each question. Read aloud your answer. Pause at each comma.**

Grammar Practice

Index

A
Action verbs, 42–43
Adjectives
   Adjectives, 36–37
   Adjectives that compare (*-er, -est, more, most*),
      40–41
   Articles (*a, an, the*), 38–39
Adjectives that compare (*-er, -est, more, most*),
   40–41
Adverbs, 56–57
Apostrophes
   in plural possessive nouns, 28–29
   proofreading for, 2–3, 8–11
   in singular possessive nouns, 26–27
   in troublesome words, 58–59, 60–61
Articles (*a, an, the*), 38–39

B
***Be*, verb forms of,** 54–55

C
Capitalization
   proofreading for, 2–3, 8–11
   of proper nouns, 20–21
   of sentences, 12–13
Commands, 12–13
Commas
   with introductory words, 62–63
   proofreading for, 2–3, 8–11
   in a series, 62–63
Common nouns, 18–19
Contractions, use of
   it's, 60–61
   they're, 60–61
   you're, 58–59
Cooperative learning, 13, 15, 17, 19, 21, 23, 25, 29,
   33, 41, 43, 45, 47, 53, 57, 59, 63

E
End marks
   See Sentences, kinds of; Punctuation.
Exclamations, 12–13

G
Games/Activities
   13, 15, 17, 19, 21, 23, 25, 27, 29, 31, 33, 35, 37, 39,
   41, 43, 45, 47, 49, 51, 53, 55, 57, 59, 61, 63

H
Helping verbs, 44–45, 52–53

I
Introductory words and commas, 62–63
Irregular plural nouns, 24–25
Irregular verbs, 50–51, 52–53
Its, it's, 60–61

K
Kinds of sentences, 2–3, 8–11, 12–13

M
Main and helping verbs, 44–45, 52–53
Mechanics
   See Capitalization; Punctuation.

N
Nouns
   common, 18–19
   irregular plural, 24–25
   plural possessive, 28–29
   proper, 20–21
   regular plural, 22–23
   singular and plural, 22–23, 24–25
   singular possessive, 26–27

O
Object pronouns, 34–35

P
Past-time verbs, 48–49
Plural possessive nouns, 28–29
Predicates, 16–17
Present-time verbs, 46–47
Pronouns
   object, 34–35
   singular and plural, 30–31
   subject, 32–33

Index

Proofreading, 2–11
    Capitalization and
    Punctuation, 2–3, 8–11
    Spelling, 4–5, 8–11
    Usage, 6–7, 8–11
Proper nouns, 20–21
Punctuation
    apostrophe in possessive nouns, 26–27, 28–29
    end marks in sentences, 12–13
    after introductory words, 62–63
    proofreading for, 2–3, 8–11
    series comma, 62–63
    with troublesome words, 58–59, 60–61

Q
Questions, 12–13

R
Regular plural nouns, 22–23

S
Sentence parts, 14–15, 16–17
Sentences, kinds of, 2–3, 8–11, 12–13
Series comma, 62–63
Singular and plural nouns, 22–23, 24–25
Singular and plural pronouns, 30–31
Singular possessive nouns, 26–27
Spelling, 4–5, 8–11, 22–23, 24–25, 52–53, 58–59, 60–61

Statements, 12–13
Subject pronouns, 32–33
Subjects, 14–15

T
Tenses, 46–49
Their, there, they're, **60–61**
To, too, two, **8–11, 58–59**
Troublesome words
    it's, its, 60–61
    their, there, they're, 60–61
    to, too, two, 58–59
    your, you're, 58–59

U
Usage, 6–7, 8–11, 58–59, 60–61

V
Verbs
    action, 42–43
    be, 54–55
    irregular, 50–51, 52–53
    main/helping, 44–45, 52–53
    past-time, 48–49
    present-time, 46–47

Y
Your, you're, **58–59**